CW00376816

CRUISING GUIDE
TO INNS AND TAVERNS
NORFOLK BROADS
Millennium Edition

by

ROSE LEWIS

British Library Cataloguing in Publication Data
Lewis, Rose

Cruising Guide to Inns and Taverns. Norfolk Broads.
A catalogue record for this book is available from the British Library.

ISBN: 0 9515467 7 5

PUBS WHICH ARE MORE THAN HALF A MILE FROM THE RIVER ARE NOT INCLUDED.

ALL   CRUISING   TIMES   AND   DISTANCES   ARE APPROXIMATE.

SUMMER TRADING TIMES ARE GENERALLY FROM WHITSUN TO MID SEPTEMBER.

BECAUSE OF THE NEW LAWS REGARDING FACILITIES FOR CHILDREN IT IS BEST TO TELEPHONE   AHEAD WHERE THE DESCRIPTION STATES "CHILDREN ARE WELCOME".

FRONT COVER: Approaching Wroxham Bridge
                                              from Coltishall
BACK COVER: Map of the Norfolk Broads

Photographs © C W Rose - September 2000

PUBLISHED BY:
Rosec Publications
135 Church Road
Shoeburyness
Essex SS3 9EZ
www.rosec.co.uk
Email: NB@rosec.co.uk

PRINTED IN GREAT BRITAIN BY:
AllStar Services Ltd (Digital Printers)
25 Forward Drive
Christchurch Business Centre
Harrow
HA3 8NT
www.allstar.co.uk
Email: sales@allstar.co.uk

MY THANKS TO:

HOSEASONS AND HORIZON CRAFT FOR THEIR HELP WITH BOAT HIRE.

MY LOVE TO:

MY MOTHER, FOR LAUGHTER AND LINE DRAWINGS.

CHRIS, MY HUSBAND, FOR BEING MAGNANIMOUS OVER MISSED MEALS, TAKING PHOTOGRAPHS AND DRAWING MAPS WHILST MAKING MOLEHILLS OUT OF ALL MY MOUNTAINS AND MANAGING TO MANOEUVRE AND MOOR WHILST NOT MENTIONING MY NAVIGATIONAL MISHAPS.

THE AUTHOR AND PUBLISHERS WELCOME ANY COMMENTS FROM THEIR READERS, GOOD OR BAD. PLEASE SEE THE FRONT PAGE OF THIS BOOK. IF YOU WISH TO ORDER FUTURE BOOKS, CD-ROMS OR JUST 'AREAS' IN THIS SERIES WE OFFER SECURE ORDERING FACILITIES ON OUR WEB SITE. SAVE MONEY AND BENEFIT THE R.N.L.I. BY ORDERING FROM OUR SITE OR DIRECT FROM US.

VISIT OUR SITE AT WWW.ROSEC.CO.UK TO VOTE FOR YOUR FAVOURITE PUB - OR EMAIL YOUR COMMENTS TO NB@ROSEC.CO.UK. OUR CUSTOMERS ARE VALUABLE TO US AND WE ARE ALWAYS INTERESTED IN *YOUR* VIEWS.

ROSEC PUBLICATIONS
135 CHURCH ROAD
SHOEBURYNESS
ESSEX SS3 9EZ
www.rosec.co.uk
Email: NB@rosec.co.uk

INTRODUCTION

Unlike the roadways of Britain there are no signposts on the waterways of the Norfolk Broads, one cannot travel after dark and it can take a fair while to "pull up at a pub".

For those who enjoy a decent drink and a good meal in congenial surroundings this river by river guide allows you to see at a glance the choices of venue open to you, the moorings available and the distances and times between your destination, wherever you may find yourself.

After several attempts to navigate my way via various maps and advertisements in an endeavour to discover the welcoming hostelry that must surely be round the next bend in the river, I wrote this Guide - if only to help others "in the same boat".

There are, again, many changes in this Millennium Edition. For the benefit of new holiday makers, and because of numerous letters received, I have included more detail for the routes and rivers which I trust everyone will benefit from. Over the years some of the pubs have closed down or been converted. I hope that the new pubs in this book (as well as those that remain) will bring you many happy hours and I can only reiterate what I always say, in my Cruising Guides:

"Have a marvellous holiday and good luck with steering your bedroom to the bar"!

Rose Lewis
September 2000

THE RIVER ANT - DISTANCES AND TIMINGS

MOUTH OF THE ANT TO NEATISHEAD, WAYFORD BRIDGE, DILHAM, SUTTON STAITHE AND STALHAM

MOUTH OF ANT TO LUDHAM BRIDGE = 1 MILE - 20 MINUTES
LUDHAM BRIDGE TO NEATISHEAD = 5 MILES - 1 HOUR
NEATISHEAD TO STALHAM OR SUTTON STAITHE = 3 MILES - 45 MINUTES
NEATISHEAD TO WAYFORD BRIDGE = 3 MILES - 45 MINUTES
WAYFORD BRIDGE TO STALHAM OR SUTTON STAITHE = 3 MILES - 45 MINUTES
WAYFORD BRIDGE TO DILHAM = 1 MILE - 20 MINUTES

DILHAM, WAYFORD BRIDGE, STALHAM, SUTTON STAITHE AND NEATISHEAD TO MOUTH OF THE ANT

DILHAM TO WAYFORD BRIDGE = 1 MILE - 20 MINUTES
WAYFORD BRIDGE TO NEATISHEAD = 3 MILES - 45 MINUTES
STALHAM OR SUTTON STAITHE TO WAYFORD BRIDGE = 3 MILES - 45 MINUTES
STALHAM OR SUTTON STAITHE TO NEATISHEAD = 3 MILES - 45 MINUTES
NEATISHEAD TO LUDHAM BRIDGE = 5 MILES - 1 HOUR
LUDHAM BRIDGE TO MOUTH OF ANT = 1 MILE - 20 MINUTES

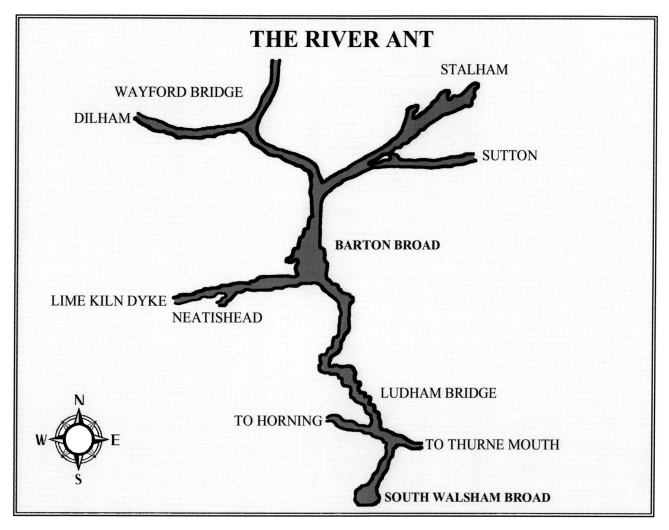

THE RIVER ANT

STALHAM

WAYFORD BRIDGE

DILHAM

SUTTON

BARTON BROAD

LIME KILN DYKE

NEATISHEAD

LUDHAM BRIDGE

TO HORNING

TO THURNE MOUTH

N
W E
S

SOUTH WALSHAM BROAD

RIVER ANT

AN EXTREMELY POPULAR RIVER DURING THE FISHING SEASON. THE MOUTH OF THE RIVER ANT LIES BETWEEN, AND ON THE OPPOSITE SIDE TO, RANWORTH BROAD AND SOUTH WALSHAM BROAD ON THE BURE. AT LUDHAM BRIDGE YOU WILL FIND GOOD MOORINGS TO YOUR RIGHT AND LEFT, AND LUDHAM BRIDGE SERVICES, ON THE RIGHT BANK, IS A GOOD PLACE FOR VICTUALS.

CRUISING UPSTREAM YOU WILL PASS HOW HILL NATURE RESERVE ON YOUR RIGHT. HERE YOU WILL FIND TOAD HOLE COTTAGE WHERE YOU CAN BUY TICKETS FOR THE "ELECTRIC EEL", A NOISELESS BOAT FROM WHICH YOU CAN SEE THE NUMEROUS WILDLIFE ON THE WATER TRAIL.

CROSSING BARTON BROAD, AS YOU GO UPSTREAM, KEEP ALL RED STAKES TO YOUR LEFT, AND TO YOUR RIGHT WHEN RETURNING. YOU CAN PASS EITHER SIDE OF PLEASURE HILL ISLAND WHICH IS SOON TO BE ENTIRELY REBUILT AS A LANDMARK. TO CRUISE TO NEATISHEAD KEEP TO THE LEFT AS YOU ENTER THE BROAD AND TAKE THE FIRST MAIN LEFT FORK. TO VISIT BARTON TURF GO ACROSS THE BROAD AND TAKE THE LEFT FORK WHERE INDICATED. TO GO TO WAYFORD BRIDGE (HEIGHT AT HIGH WATER 7') AND DILHAM, KEEP TO THE RIGHT FORK. FOR STALHAM OR SUTTON BEAR RIGHT WHERE INDICATED FURTHER UPSTREAM BEARING LEFT FOR STALHAM, RIGHT FOR SUTTON.

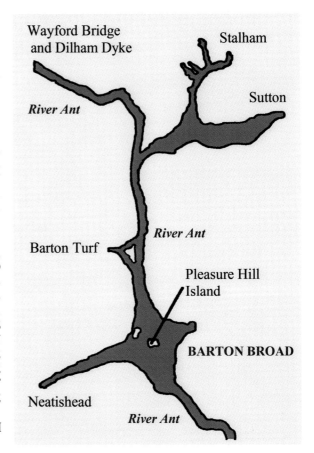

NEATISHEAD

BARTON ANGLER COUNTRY INN TEL: (01692) 630740

5 MILES FROM LUDHAM BRIDGE - 1 HOUR
3 MILES TO STALHAM OR SUTTON STAITHE - 45 MINUTES
3 MILES TO WAYFORD BRIDGE - 45 MINUTES

MOORINGS: There are several at "Gay's Staithe" just before steering round to Lime Kiln Dyke. Mostly stern on. No fees. Distance to the hotel is 200 yards.

SUMMER:	11.30 to 11
WINTER:	Noon to 2.30 and 7 to 11
SUNDAY:	Noon to 10.30

BEERS:	Greene King, IPA, XS, Abbot and Murphys
LAGERS:	Carling Black Label and Stella Artois
SPECIALITIES:	Lemon Sole. Cromer Crab. Roast Partridge. Tuna Steaks. Fiery Chilli.
SUNDAY LUNCH:	Roasts - £5.95
BAR MEALS:	Noon to 2 and 6.30 to 9

DINING FACILITIES: Seating anywhere. Times as above. Typical cost of three course meal for two with wine: £30.

CARDS: All main cards accepted.

An old rectory house set in four acres of landscaped gardens featuring many varieties of Azaleas and Rhododendrons. An A La Carte restaurant is available on Saturday evenings and there is a non-smoking conservatory.

Wheelchair access is via the front door. No dogs, except in gardens. Full hotel accommodation is provided with two rooms boasting four-poster beds. Is there a ghost in Bedroom No. 1?

Lord Nelson visited as a boy and learnt to sail on nearby Barton Broad. Rowing boats may be hired from here and there is good fishing in the area.

NEATISHEAD

THE WHITE HORSE   TEL: (01692) 630828

5 MILES FROM LUDHAM BRIDGE - 1 HOUR
3 MILES TO STALHAM OR SUTTON STAITHE - 45 MINUTES
3 MILES TO WAYFORD BRIDGE - 45 MINUTES

MOORINGS: Several, side on, in Lime Kiln Dyke. These are free for 24 hours and are 300 yards from the pub. Torches required at night.

SUMMER:	All day
WINTER:	All day
SUNDAY:	Noon to 10.30
BEERS:	Greene King, IPA, Tolly Original and Old Strong, Adnams and Broadside
LAGERS:	Stella, Carlsberg and XXXX
SPECIALITIES:	Local Sausages. Beef and Ale pie. Vegetable Wellington. Portuguese Sardines in garlic.
SUNDAY LUNCH:	Main Menu. Roasts in Winter for £4.95
BAR MEALS:	12 to 2.30 and 6.30 to 8.30

DINING FACILITIES: Seating in any of the 3 bars (one of which is non-smoking) and terrace. Times as above. Typical cost of three course meal for two with wine: £25.

CARDS: All major cards accepted.

This 500 year old hostelry is now under new management and it's pleasing to see they have extended the opening hours. Much of the pub has been left in it's original state, with bare floors and small bars – a refreshing change in this era of plastic and chrome.

Real ale, good food, darts, cribbage, pool, table football and a warm welcome. Food and wine tastings in the winter and live music during regattas and holiday weekends. Dogs allowed and children also, but not in the public bar. Limited facilities for the disabled.

Lime Kiln Dyke is an attractive wooded area with a turning basin at its apex.

WAYFORD BRIDGE

WAYFORD BRIDGE HOTEL TEL: (01692) 582414

3 MILES FROM NEATISHEAD - 45 MINUTES
3 MILES TO STALHAM OR SUTTON STAITHE - 45 MINUTES
1 MILE TO DILHAM - 20 MINUTES

MOORINGS: Numerous on both banks either side of the bridge. A nominal fee is payable after 5.30 if staying overnight on the West bank. Distance to the pub is 50 to 300 yards. Torches useful at night.

SUMMER:	All day - July, August and September
WINTER:	11 to 2..30 and 5.30 to 11
SUNDAY:	12 to 2..30 & 6 to 10.30.Summer as above
BEERS:	Stones, Worthington, Murphys, Adnams, Caffreys, M&B Mild, Guinness & Guests
LAGERS:	Stella, Carling and Grolsch
SPECIALITIES:	Fresh Fish and Charcoal Grilled Specials. Tagliatelle Carbonara. Children's and Vegetarian Menus.
SUNDAY LUNCH:	Roasts - £4.95
BAR MEALS:	Noon to 2 and 6 to 9 (Sunday 6.30 to 9)

DINING FACILITIES: Seating for over 100. Times as above. Typical cost of three course meal for two with wine: £30.

CARDS: All main cards except Amex.

Once known as the Woodfarm Inn this has recently been taken over and turned into a lovely hotel. There are 12, very large, en-suite rooms with those on the ground floor suitable for people with mobility problems.

A warm welcome awaits in the bar with it's plush seating and mellow cream walls which set off the oak beams, farming implements and copper canopies over the fireplaces..

Two non-smoking restaurants (Bistro and A La Carte) and a circular bar, where meals are also available, command excellent views of the river. Breakfast for the river traveller at £6.50 per head. Good for fishing all round this area.

DILHAM DYKE

THE CROSS KEYS   TEL: (01692) 536398

1 MILE FROM WAYFORD BRIDGE - 20 MINUTES

MOORINGS: There are 4 to 5 side on and there is no fee. Make your way up the grass embankment and turn left at the Bridge. The pub is a five minute walk away.

SUMMER:	11.30 to 3 and 6 to 11
WINTER:	Noon to 2.30 and 7 to 11
SUNDAY:	Noon to 4 and 6 to 10.30

Times may change so please telephone ahead

BEERS:	Adnams, Greene King, Tetleys, Murphys and Calders
LAGERS:	Stella Artois and Carlsberg
SPECIALITIES:	Honey Roast Ham. Chicken Kiev. Spaghetti Bolognese. Peach Melba.
SUNDAY LUNCH:	Main Menu available
BAR MEALS:	Noon to 2 and 7 to 9

DINING FACILITIES: Seating anywhere in the pub. Times as above. Typical cost of two course meal for two with wine: £16.

CARDS: Cheque with bankers cards.

One of the more delightful village inns with one bar overlooking the bowling green. Pleasant hospitality and a convivial atmosphere make this an agreeable stopover for the traveller who seeks that away from it all mood, without mooring in the middle of a Broad.

The only music comes from a juke box. Pool and darts are provided in the saloon bar. Children alllowed in the garden. Dogs on leads, please.

An extremely attractive 3 mph stretch of river leads to the end of navigation on the River Ant. Please take care in your approach along this stretch to avoid wash against the riverside gardens of private houses. Watch for Kingfishers!

STALHAM

THE MAIDS HEAD   TEL: (01692) 580200

3 MILES FROM NEATISHEAD - 45 MINUTES
3 MILES TO WAYFORD BRIDGE - 45 MINUTES

MOORINGS: Numerous free areas in and around the various boatyards and Stalham Dyke. The pub is the first one you will come to, on your left, in the High Street which is a five minute stroll away.

SUMMER:	All day
WINTER:	All day
SUNDAY:	Noon to 10.30
BEERS:	Guest Ales, John Smiths Smooth and Caffreys
LAGERS:	Stella, Fosters and Carlsberg
SPECIALITIES:	Beef and Ale Casserole. Lasagne. Spare Ribs. Vegetarian specials and Children's Menu.
SUNDAY LUNCH:	Main Menu available. Roast Chicken or Beef for £5.95, including choice of sweet.
BAR MEALS:	Noon to 2.30 and 6 to 9.30

DINING FACILITIES: Seating for 100 anywhere in pub or gardens. Times as for bar meals. Average cost for two for a three course meal with wine: £20

CARDS:	Cheque with bankers card.

New for this edition, a family pub which offers a beer garden, a children's games room, pool table and live entertainment at weekends.

An attractive 600 year old pub with a cosy saloon bar and a split level, L-shaped, dining area with plush seating and a copper canopy over the fireplace.

*There are **no** non-smoking areas and dogs are welcome.*

The market, which is on Tuesdays, is held behind the pub.

STALHAM

THE KINGFISHER HOTEL   TEL: (01692) 581974

3 MILES FROM NEATISHEAD - 45 MINUTES
3 MILES TO WAYFORD BRIDGE - 45 MINUTES

MOORINGS: Numerous free areas in and around the various boatyards and Stalham Dyke. The pub is at the top of the High Street - approximately 1/4 mile from the moorings.

SUMMER:	11 to 2.30 and 6 to 11
WINTER:	11 to 2.30 and 6 to 11
SUNDAY:	12 to 2.30 and 7 to 10.30

BEERS:	Adnams, Bass, Stones, Guinness and Caffreys
LAGERS:	Carlsberg and Carling Black Label

SPECIALITIES: Whole pan fried Sole coated with Almonds. Tiger Prawns. Lamb Chops in Port and Rosemary sauce.

SUNDAY LUNCH: Roasts - £4.95

BAR MEALS: Noon to 2 and 7 to 9

DINING FACILITIES: Seating for 40. Noon to 2 and 7 to 9. Typical cost of three course meal for two with wine: £35.

CARDS: All major cards except Amex.

Set in the heart of this small market town the Kingfisher, with its en-suite bedrooms and pleasant decor, is well known for its extensive menus - specialising in local seafood dishes.

There is one bar and no games or music are provided - making this a refreshing change for some.

The landscaped gardens are especially attractive. Dogs welcome. Children are allowed in the bar and no-smoking restaurant and there are good facilities for the disabled, with ramp access into the hotel.

SUTTON STAITHE

SUTTON STAITHE HOTEL TEL: (01692) 580244

2 MILES FROM NEATISHEAD – 40 MINUTES
2 MILES TO WAYFORD BRIDGE – 40 MINUTES

MOORINGS: These are side on and plentiful along the left hand bank as you approach the Staithe. There is no charge for the first 24 hours and the pub is 100 to 300 yards along the towpath and through a small copse - or right outside.

SUMMER:	11 to 11
WINTER:	11 to 11
SUNDAY:	Noon to 10.30

BEERS:	Beamish, M&B Mild, John Smiths Smooth, Polly's Folly & Courage Best
LAGERS:	Holsten Export and Fosters

SPECIALITIES: Rainbow Trout. Chargrilled Steaks. Chilli Chicken Dippers. Whitebait. Children's and Vegetarian Menus.

SUNDAY LUNCH: Carvery - £5.95. £2.95 for children

BAR MEALS: Noon to 2 and 6.30 to 9

DINING FACILITIES: Seating for 50. Times as above. Average cost of three course meal for two with wine: £30.

CARDS: All main cards accepted.

A traditional country pub and hotel with low oak beams, brass ships' lamps, soft lights, open fireplaces and low background music.

The main bar leads into a further room, with flagged floors. The restaurant, with its antique dressers, is separately situated and boasts an extensive A La Carte menu. A smaller, non-smoking, restaurant is available.

Full hotel accommodation. Dogs allowed. Good access for the disabled. Children are welcome and there are Conference facilities for 200. Disco on Friday nights in the summer.

Nearby is the Broads Museum and famous Sutton Windmill with its nine floors, built in 1789.

THE RIVER THURNE - DISTANCES AND TIMINGS

MOUTH OF THE THURNE TO HICKLING, HORSEY AND WEST SOMERTON

MOUTH OF THE THURNE TO THURNE = 1/2 MILE - 15 MINUTES
THURNE TO WOMACK STAITHE = 2 MILES - 20 MINUTES
WOMACK STAITHE TO POTTER HEIGHAM = 2 MILES - 20 MINUTES
POTTER HEIGHAM TO HICKLING BROAD = 4 1/2 MILES - 1 HOUR
POTTER HEIGHAM TO WEST SOMERTON = 4 1/2 MILES - 1 HOUR
POTTER HEIGHAM TO HORSEY MERE = 4 MILES - 1 HOUR

HICKLING, HORSEY AND WEST SOMERTON TO MOUTH OF THE THURNE

HORSEY MERE TO POTTER HEIGHAM = 4 MILES - 1 HOUR
WEST SOMERTON TO POTTER HEIGHAM = 4 1/2 MILES - 1 HOUR
HICKLING BROAD TO POTTER HEIGHAM = 4 1/2 MILES - 1 HOUR
POTTER HEIGHAM TO WOMACK STAITHE = 2 MILES - 20 MINUTES
WOMACK STAITHE TO THURNE = 2 MILES - 20 MINUTES
THURNE TO MOUTH OF THE THURNE = 1/2 MILE - 15 MINUTES

THE RIVER THURNE

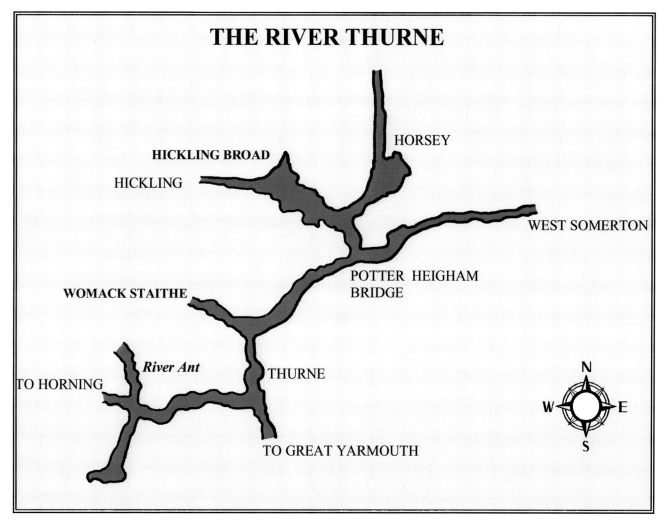

THE RIVER THURNE

JUST PAST THE MOUTH OF THE THURNE IS ST. BENET'S LEVEL WINDPUMP ON YOUR LEFT AND THURNE DYKE WINDPUMP ON YOUR RIGHT, WHICH IS OPEN DURING DAYLIGHT HOURS IN THE SUMMER.

IF YOU VISIT WOMACK STAITHE (WALK FROM MOORINGS TO LUDHAM) YOU'LL SEE THE NORFOLK WHERRY TRUST. ON UP TO POTTER HEIGHAM PASSING SMALL WATERSIDE CHALETS, SOME WITH EXTREMELY PRETTY FACADES AND GARDENS. IN PARTICULAR LOOK OUT FOR AN UNUSUAL LOOKING COTTAGE ON YOUR LEFT, PURPORTED TO ONCE HAVE BEEN THE TOP OF A HELTER-SKELTER RIDE AT GREAT YARMOUTH!

POTTER HEIGHAM, OF COURSE, IS FAMOUS FOR IT'S BRIDGE (PICTURED ABOVE), "BRIDGE STORES" AND LATHAMS. AT THE BRIDGE YOU MUST WAIT FOR THE PILOT IF YOU WISH TO TRAVEL FURTHER AS THE HEIGHT OF THE BRIDGE IS ONLY 6'9" AT THE CENTRE POINT AT HIGH WATER. ONCE UNDER THE BRIDGE YOU'LL PASS 'HIGH'S MILL' ON YOUR RIGHT. OPPOSITE THIS IS 'CANDLE DYKE' LEADING TO HEIGHAM SOUND AND THEN, VIA A LEFT HAND FORK, HICKLING BROAD. TAKE THE RIGHT FORK FOR 'MEADOW DYKE' WHICH LEADS TO HORSEY MERE.

IF YOU ARE GOING DIRECTLY TO WEST SOMERTON KEEP ON PAST THE TURNING TO CANDLE DYKE AND STAY ON THE MAIN RIVER TO SOMERTON STAITHE.

THURNE

THE LION   TEL: (01692) 670796

1/2 MILE FROM THURNE MOUTH - 15 MINUTES
2 MILES TO WOMACK STAITHE - 20 MINUTES

MOORINGS: Approximately 30 side on. There is no charge for mooring on the left hand bank but a small fee is requested for those on the right. The distance to the pub is 100 to 300 yards. Torches may be useful at night.

SUMMER:	11 to 11
WINTER:	12 to 2 and 7 to 11
SUNDAY:	12 to 3 and 7 to 10.30

BEERS: Boddingtons, Caffreys, Flowers, Adnams, Wherry, Guinness and Guests
LAGERS: Heineken and Stella Artois

SPECIALITIES: Greenlip Mussells. Sirloin Steak. Chicken, Beef and Veg. Yorkies. South American Cajun. Thai Curries.

SUNDAY LUNCH: Roasts - £4.95 for two courses

BAR MEALS: 11 to 2 and 6 to 9

DINING FACILITIES: Seating for 200 inside and out. Times as above. Average cost of three course meal for two with wine: £25.

CARDS: All main cards except Amex.

The Lion welcomed new owners in September 2000. A purpose built restaurant with smoking and no-smoking areas and function facilities together with a Games Room are now provided.

An old Victorian House with traditional decor and open fires, pool table, amusements and a family room. Soft background music. Dogs are allowed - on leads please. Full facilities for the disabled.

A take away Menu is available and the pub's Gift Shop is just across the road. A windmill and a restored windpump stand near the entrance to the dyke leading up to the pub.

WOMACK STAITHE

THE KINGS ARMS TEL: (01692) 678386

2 MILES FROM THURNE - 20 MINUTES
2 MILES TO POTTER HEIGHAM - 20 MINUTES

MOORINGS: These are numerous and stern on. Look out for the Norfolk Wherry "Albion" on your way. A five minute walk takes you along the footpath into the village of Ludham. There is a small fee and quite a few berths are taken up by private cruisers.

SUMMER:	All day
WINTER:	All day
SUNDAY:	Noon to 10.30
BEERS:	Tetleys, Greene King IPA, Guinness, Abbot, Ruddles, John Smiths & Caffreys
LAGERS:	Fosters, Stella Artois and Carlsberg
SPECIALITIES:	Garlic Chicken. Half a Roast Duck. Beef in Black Bean sauce. Red Snapper. Steak and Onion Pie. Vegetarian meals.
SUNDAY LUNCH:	Roasts - £5.25 and main menu available
BAR MEALS:	Noon to 3 and 6 to 9

DINING FACILITIES: Seating for 24. Times as above. Typical cost of three course meal for two with wine: £30.

CARDS: Main cards (£10 minimum purchase) plus Cashback.

A real country pub which is popular with holiday makers and local residents alike. The interior is well decorated featuring an L-shaped saloon bar, with pool table, juke box and darts, which leads to a new Games Room. Sky TV. Take away Pizzas.

A small and pleasantly cosy bar, to your left offers non-smoking restaurant facilities.

Nearby is the 14th Century St. Catherine's Church which is one of the largest in Norfolk and boasts an impressive interior.

How Hill Nature Reserve is within walking distance if you do not wish to make your way by river to the moorings provided on the River Ant.

POTTER HEIGHAM

THE FALGATE INN   TEL: (01692) 670003

**2 MILES FROM WOMACK STAITHE - 20 MINUTES
4 1/2 MILES TO HICKLING AND WEST SOMERTON - 1 HOUR**

MOORINGS: Both alongside the bank and in the basin. There is no charge and the distance to the pub is 800 yards. Turn left at the Bridge and go past a small estate. Torches useful at night.

SUMMER:	11 to 3 and 6 to 11
WINTER:	11 to 3 and 6 to 11
SUNDAY:	12 to 3 and 7 to 10.30

BEERS: Boddingtons, Tetleys, Greene King IPA and Guest Ales

LAGERS: Stella Artois and Carlsberg

SPECIALITIES: HomeMade Pate. Moules Marinieres. Lemon Sole. Fillet & T-Bone Steaks. Vegetarian menu. No GM Products!

SUNDAY LUNCH: Roasts - £4.95. Very popular so it may be wise to book ahead

BAR MEALS: Noon to 2.30 and 7 to 9

DINING FACILITIES: Seating for 26. Times as above Average cost of three course meal for two with wine: £35.

CARDS: All main cards accepted. Minimum purchase of £15.

Worth the ten minute walk - so treat yourself! A large old village Inn which was once a Toll House. In the lounge bar the focal point is the fine Tudor fireplace surrounded by horse brasses.

The A La Carte restaurant is intimate and tastefully decorated and it would be a shame to miss out, both on the fabulous food and the Falgate's own excellent wines.

A family room, dartboard and beer garden are provided. Dogs allowed in bar or garden only. En-suite rooms and full English breakfast.

On 27th February 1993 the thatched roof of the pub caught fire and the Falgate only re-opened in November of that year.

HICKLING BROAD

PLEASURE BOAT INN
TEL: (01692) 598211

4 1/2 MILES FROM POTTER HEIGHAM - 1 HOUR
2 MILES TO WEST SOMERTON OR HORSEY - 30 MINUTES

MOORINGS: These are plentiful and side on. There is no charge and the pub is 50 to 300 yards away - dependant on where you are moored.

SUMMER:	All day
WINTER:	All day
SUNDAY:	Noon to 10.30
BEERS:	John Smiths, IPA, Courage Best, Guinness and Guest Beers
LAGERS:	Fosters and Stella Artois

SPECIALITIES: Selection of Seafood and a range of Vegetarian and Home-Cooked food. 'Special' nights on Thursdays.

SUNDAY LUNCH: Roasts - £4.95 plus Main Menu

BAR MEALS: Noon to 2.30 and 7 to 9

DINING FACILITIES: Seating for 50 inside and 70 outside. Noon to 2.30 and 6.30 to 9.30. Typical cost of three course meal for two with wine: £23.

CARDS: Main cards accepted

A change of ownership in May 2000. A popular pub with large and airy rooms and good facilities for the disabled. There is a play area for children and dogs are allowed.

Holidaymakers will enjoy themselves here as there is a free and easy atmosphere. A good A La Carte menu is now available. Smoking allowed.

Hickling Broad is the largest lake in Broadlands and was designated as a National Nature Reserve in 1945.

A water trail begins near the pub where it is possible to travel on a replica of a traditional reed-carrying boat known as a "lighter".

WEST SOMERTON

THE LION   TEL: (01493) 393289

**4 1/2 MILES FROM POTTER HEIGHAM - 1 HOUR
2 MILES TO HICKLING BROAD AND HORSEY - 30 MINUTES**

MOORINGS: There is room for approximately 40 side on along the dyke, bearing right. A charge of £2 is levied by the river authority. The distance to the pub is 400 yards going up the hill and around the field. Torches required at night.

SUMMER:	11 to 3.30 and 6 to 11
WINTER:	11 to 3.30 and 6 to 11
SUNDAY:	12 to 3.30 and 7 to 10.30
BEERS:	Greene King IPA, Abbot, Guinness and selected Traditional Ales
LAGERS:	Carling Black Label and Grolsch
SPECIALITIES:	T-Bone Steaks. Lasagne. King Prawns in Garlic Butter. Knickerbocker Glory. Tiramisu Ice Cream.
SUNDAY LUNCH:	Main menu available. Roasts in Winter
BAR MEALS:	11 to 3 and 6 to 9

DINING FACILITIES: Seating for 40. Times as above. Average cost of three course meal for two with wine: £30.

CARDS: All main cards accepted.

This Freehouse enjoys agreeable hospitality and comfort. It is tastefully decorated and inglenook seating makes for privacy if you feel so inclined.

Willing and cheerful staff give lively service in the lounge and saloon bars and the local residents are happy to mingle and chat with visiting river travellers.

A pool table is in use in the Winter months and a dartboard is available all year round. Dogs are welcome and there is also a children's room.

HORSEY MERE

THE NELSON HEAD   TEL: (01493) 393378

4 ½ MILES FROM POTTER HEIGHAM - 1 HOUR

MOORINGS: Room for 50 boats anchored side on. There is a small fee and the pub is half a mile from the Staithe.

SUMMER:	11 to 2.30 and 6 to 11
WINTER:	11 to 2.30 and 7 to 11
SUNDAY:	Noon to 3 and 7 to 10.30

BEERS:	Greene King, Woodfordes Wherry and Revenge and Whitbread Mild
LAGERS:	Stella Artois and Carlsberg

SPECIALITIES: Smoked Mackerel. Basque Chicken. Locally made sausages. Fillet Steaks. Vegetarian and Children's meals. Twitchers' Lunches!

SUNDAY LUNCH: Roasts - £6.25

BAR MEALS: Noon to 2 and 6 to 9

DINING FACILITIES: Seating for 23. Times as above. Average cost of three course meal for two with wine: £30

CARDS: Cheque with bankers card.

Tall people duck your heads! The doorway to this old, recently refurbished Freehouse is only 5'.8". Dogs allowed anywhere apart from dining room.

The fireplace in the lounge is large enough to sit in and the bar area has a wealth of brass, copper and ships' memorabilia.

The small, non-smoking, dining room boasts an open fire in Winter and families are welcome. A Marquee bar is available for inclement weather.

Large beer gardens surround the pub which is situated in the centre of a National Trust estate, half a mile from the beach and half a mile from the fully restored Horsey windmill.

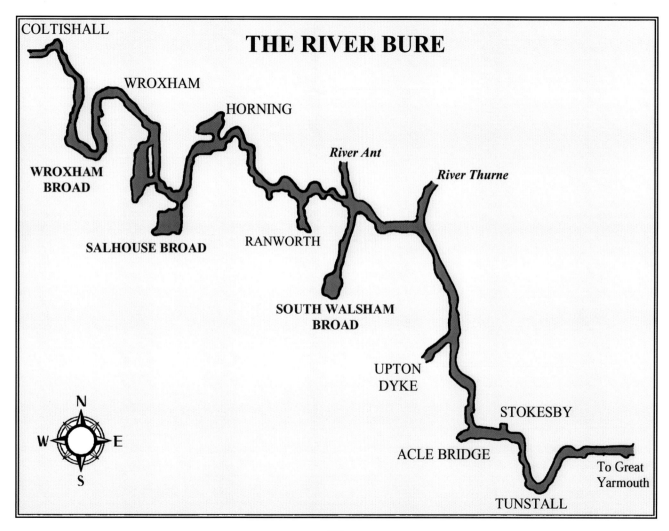

THE RIVER BURE - DISTANCES AND TIMINGS

COLTISHALL TO GREAT YARMOUTH

COLTISHALL TO WROXHAM = 4 MILES - 45 MINUTES
WROXHAM TO HORNING = 5 MILES - 1 HOUR
HORNING TO RANWORTH = 3 MILES - 30 MINUTES
RANWORTH TO THURNE MOUTH = 3 MILES - 30 MINUTES
(ANT MOUTH TO THURNE MOUTH = 2 MILES - 20 MINUTES)
THURNE MOUTH TO UPTON DYKE = 3 MILES - 30 MINUTES
UPTON DYKE TO ACLE BRIDGE = 1 MILE -20 MINUTES
ACLE BRIDGE TO STOKESBY = 2 MILES - 20 MINUTES
STOKESBY TO TUNSTALL = 2 MILES - 20 MINUTES
TUNSTALL TO GREAT YARMOUTH = 8 MILES -1 1/2 HOURS

GREAT YARMOUTH TO COLTISHALL

GREAT YARMOUTH TO TUNSTALL = 8 MILES - 1 1/2 HOURS
TUNSTALL TO STOKESBY = 2 MILES - 20 MINUTES
STOKESBY TO ACLE BRIDGE = 2 MILES - 20 MINUTES
ACLE BRIDGE TO UPTON DYKE = 1 MILE - 20 MINUTES
UPTON DYKE TO THURNE MOUTH = 3 MILES - 30 MINUTES
(THURNE MOUTH TO ANT MOUTH = 2 MILES - 20 MINUTES)
THURNE MOUTH TO RANWORTH = 3 MILES - 30 MINUTES
RANWORTH TO HORNING = 3 MILES - 30 MINUTES
HORNING TO WROXHAM = 5 MILES - 1 HOUR
WROXHAM TO COLTISHALL = 4 MILES - 45 MINUTES

THE RIVER BURE

COLTISHALL IS THE HEAD OF NAVIGATION ON THIS RIVER WHICH RUNS FOR OVER 30 MILES DOWN TO GREAT YARMOUTH. ONE OF THE PRETTIEST STRETCHES ON THE BROADS IS FROM COLTISHALL TO WROXHAM.

WROXHAM BRIDGE (BUILT IN 1614) MUST ONLY BE NAVIGATED AT LOW TIDES. (HEIGHT 7'3" AT HIGH WATER). WROXHAM IS ONE OF THE BEST PLACES TO SHOP AND FROM HERE YOU CAN VISIT WROXHAM BARNS OR TAKE A 9 MILE TRIP ON THE BURE VALLEY RAILWAY TO AYLSHAM.

BEFORE REACHING HORNING YOU PASS WROXHAM BROAD, HOVETON GREAT BROAD NATURE TRAIL, SALHOUSE BROAD AND SALHOUSE VILLAGE WHERE THERE IS AN EQUESTRIAN CENTRE. HORNING STRETCHES FOR QUITE A WAY AND YOU MAY SEE THE "SOUTHERN COMFORT" PADDLE STEAMER PLYING BACK AND FORTH BETWEEN HERE AND RANWORTH DYKE ALMOST OPPOSITE THE ANT MOUTH. THE ENTRANCE TO RANWORTH LIES THROUGH MALTHOUSE BROAD.

THE DISTANCE BETWEEN THE ANT MOUTH AND THE THURNE MOUTH IS TWO MILES. TWO MILES FURTHER ON IS THE ENTRANCE TO UPTON DYKE ON YOUR RIGHT. ACLE BRIDGE COMES NEXT AND THEN STOKESBY WITH ITS CANDLEMAKING AND MODEL CENTRE.

ON NOW TO TUNSTALL AND THE 'THREE FEATHERS' - ONCE KNOWN AS THE "STRACEY ARMS" (OVERNIGHT MOORING FEE OF £5). THIS IS THE LAST PLACE TO MOOR BEFORE THE STRETCH TO GREAT YARMOUTH (MOORINGS PICTURED ABOVE) WHERE NUMEROUS ATTRACTIONS MAY KEEP YOU ENTERTAINED FOR A WHILE. HORSE DRAWN CARRIAGES, TREASURE WORLD, CRAZY GOLF, THE HOUSE OF WAX, REGENT BOWL (TEN PIN BOWLING), WELLINGTON AND BRITANNIA PIERS, MARINA LEISURE CENTRE, PLEASURE BEACH FAIRGROUND, RIPLEY'S ODDITORIUM, THE SEA LIFE CENTRE, BUTTERFLY FARM AND MERRIVALE MODEL VILLAGE ARE ALL NEARBY. THERE ARE ALSO MANY EXCELLENT PUBS, RESTAURANTS AND BEACHES.

COLTISHALL

THE KINGS HEAD TEL: (01603) 737426

4 MILES TO WROXHAM - 45 MINUTES

MOORINGS: These are plentiful and side on. There is no charge for the first 24 hours and you will find the Kings Head tucked just behind the Rising Sun, on your left as you approach the main road.

SUMMER:	11 to 3 and 6 to 11
WINTER:	11 to 3 and 6 to 11
SUNDAY:	Noon to 10.30 May to October. Noon to 3 and 6 to 10.30 November to April

BEERS:	Adnams, Woodfordes and Courage
LAGERS:	Kronenberg, Carlsberg and Fosters

SPECIALITIES: Half a Crispy Duck with Grand Marnier sauce. Fillet Steak with Wild Mushrooms. Fillet of Cod with Button Onions and Mushrooms.

SUNDAY LUNCH: £5.95 per head plus main menu.

BAR MEALS: Noon to 2 and 7 to 9.30

DINING FACILITIES: Seating for 60. Times as above. Typical cost of three course meal for two with wine: £24.

CARDS: All main cards except Diners and Amex.

A 17th century beamed interior with Broadland antique and fishing themes running throughout the pub. Log fires are lit when it's cool.

The Restaurant which overlooks the seating provided outside and the river beyond was totally refurbished and extended in 1990. Smoking allowed.

Music is supplied by background tapes and the juke box has a decent selection of music. Dogs and children welcome. Good facilities for the disabled.

COLTISHALL

THE RISING SUN   TEL: (01603) 737440

4 MILES TO WROXHAM - 45 MINUTES

MOORINGS: Approximately 35 side on. There is no fee for the first 24 hours and the pub is 50 to 500 yards away.

SUMMER:	All day
WINTER:	11 to 3 and 6 to 11
SUNDAY:	12 to 3 and 7 to 10.30

BEERS: Theakstons Best, XB and Mild and John Smiths Smooth

LAGERS: Fosters and Kronenberg

SPECIALITIES: Theakston Battered Cod. Half a Roast Chicken. Vegetarian and Children's Menu. Steak and Kidney Pie. Steaks.

SUNDAY LUNCH: Main Course - £4.95

BAR MEALS: 11.30 to 2 and 6.30 to 9

DINING FACILITIES: Seating for 60. Meal times as above. Typical cost of three course meal for two with wine: £20.

CARDS: All main cards except Amex, plus Cashback.

Situated on an old public staithe once used by traditional Norfolk Wherries this is a well known hostelry - originally a grain store and maltings.

Smartened up externally with white paint and hanging baskets the pub still retains it's character. A rambling interior, dotted with Chesterfields, lounge chairs and interesting photographs of the old days in the two bars. Music is supplied by background tapes and pool is available. Dogs allowed except in food serving areas.

An extremely large patio lies adjacent to a play area. Children are also welcome in the Granary restaurant which overlooks the river and is a no-smoking area. A separate dining room is provided as are excellent facilities for the disabled.

COLTISHALL

THE RED LION   TEL: (01603) 737402

4 MILES TO WROXHAM - 45 MINUTES

MOORINGS: These are plentiful and side on. There is no charge for the first 24 hours. Turn left at the top of the staithe, walk past the small parade of shops in the village and you will find the pub 400 yards down the road almost opposite the church. Torches required at night.

SUMMER:	All day
WINTER:	11 to 3 and 5 to 11
SUNDAY:	Noon to 10.30

BEERS:	Abbot, Adnams, Caffreys and Couteshall Weaselpis
LAGERS:	Heineken and Stella Artois

SPECIALITIES: Steak and Kidney pie. Steak and Ale pie. Red Lion Curry. 'Specials' Board.

SUNDAY LUNCH: Roasts - £4.95 plus Main Menu

BAR MEALS: Noon to 9.30

DINING FACILITIES: Seating for 60. Food available most of the time, seven days a week. Typical cost of three course meal for two with wine: £23.

CARDS: All main cards, plus Cashback.

A quaint split level pub which was originally three Alms Houses and a very small beer house dating back to the 14th Century.

Families are sure of good food and a warm welcome. Please note that the restaurant is non-smoking. Dogs are allowed, although not in the new "soft play"childrens' area built in September 2000. Good facilites for the disabled.

The real ales available will lure the traditional beer drinkers even if they failed to take note of one of the beers mentioned above which is brewed exclusively for the Red Lion!

WROXHAM BRIDGE

KINGS HEAD HOTEL   TEL: (01603) 782429

4 MILES FROM COLTISHALL - 45 MINUTES
5 MILES TO HORNING - 1 HOUR

MOORINGS: On the Coltishall side of the bridge, on your right at the "bottom of the garden". There is no charge if you use the facilities. Alternatively - walk over from various boat yard moorings on the Wroxham side.

SUMMER:	All day
WINTER:	All day
SUNDAY:	Noon to 10.30
BEERS:	Theakstons, Directors and John Smith
LAGERS:	Holstein, Fosters and Kronenberg

SPECIALITIES: Country Carvery with a choice of three roasts. Scampi. Turkey Korma.

SUNDAY LUNCH: Carvery all day. £11.75 per head for a three course feast. £6.75 for main course.

BAR MEALS: Noon to 9 seven days a week

DINING FACILITIES: Seating for over 100. Carvery open from noon to 2 and 6 to 9 – all day on Sunday. Typical cost of three course meal for two with wine: £28.

CARDS: All major cards plus Cashback

This is a large hotel with all facilities and therefore has something for everyone. Friendly service in an informal atmosphere. Music is provided by juke boxes with light background music in the Carvery which is attractive and roomy.

Live music is provided at weekends during the summer, in the main lounge bar. There is a children's play area outside and dogs are welcome in the garden. Good facilities for the disabled.

If you'd like to try your luck at fishing (especially pike) the hotel offers special holidays, which are all inclusive, from 1st November to 16th March.

HORNING

THE SWAN HOTEL   TEL: (01692) 630316

5 MILES FROM WROXHAM - 1 HOUR
3 MILES TO RANWORTH - 30 MINUTES

MOORINGS: Approximately 10 side on. There is no charge and the hotel is across the lawns.

SUMMER: All day
WINTER: All day
SUNDAY: Noon to 10.30

BEERS: Whitbread Best, Boddingtons, Flowers Guinness, Murphys and Guest Ales

LAGERS: Stella Artois and Heineken

SPECIALITIES: Surf 'n Turf. Toad in the Hole. Salmon with Mushrooms and Shrimp sauce. Minty Lamb Chops. Vegetarian and Children's menu

SUNDAY LUNCH: Roasts - £5.99

BAR MEALS: 11 to 10. Noon to 9 on Sundays.

DINING FACILITIES: Seating for 44. Times as above Typical cost of three course meal for two with wine: £25.

CARDS: All main cards accepted.

Long and rambling this hotel was built in 1897. Generous seating is provided in the gardens which front onto the river. Catch the 'Southern Comfort' Paddle Steamer from outside the hotel.

Settle yourself anywhere for a meal. An off-set dining area is offered which is a no-smoking area. Pool and darts are provided and there is a games area. Dogs are allowed in the gardens. Family entertainment is regularly organised. Very good facilities for the disabled. Excellent 'specials' blackboard.

En Suite rooms are available for bed and breakfast. Please telephone ahead for details.

HORNING

PETERSFIELD HOUSE HOTEL TEL: (01692) 630741

5 1/2 MILES FROM WROXHAM - 1 HOUR
2 1/2 MILES TO RANWORTH - 30 MINUTES

MOORINGS: Three to four side on at the end of the gardens. Walk across the bridge (usually floodlit at night), over the road and up the slope into the bar. Overnight moorings are only for those using the restaurant. Torches useful at night.

SUMMER: All day
WINTER: All day
SUNDAY: Noon to 10.30

BEERS: Adnams and Bitburger
LAGERS: Stella Artois and Carlsberg

SPECIALITIES: Scottish Smoked Salmon. Minted Lamb Kofta. Dover Sole. Veal Cutlets. Lobster. Constantly changing menu with all meals being freshly prepared.

SUNDAY LUNCH: £13.95

BAR MEALS: Noon to 2. None in the evening

DINING FACILITIES: Seating for 60. 7 to 9.30. Typical cost of a three course meal for two with wine: £45.

CARDS: All main cards accepted.

Not previously featured this lovely old hotel and restaurant is a must for the discerning holidaymaker.

Set in two acres of beautifully tended landscaped gardens the hotel was built in 1923 as a private residence, then sold to a couple from Petersfield, hence it's name.

The restaurant, where smoking is allowed after 9.30 p.m. and smart, casual wear is preferred, is a connoisseur's delight with over 60 fine wines to choose from.

Dogs not allowed in public rooms. Good facilities for the disabled. Own fishing amenities. Saturday night dinner dances. Look out for 'Charlie'!

HORNING

THE FERRY INN   TEL: (01692) 630259

5 ½ MILES FROM WROXHAM - 1 HOUR
2 ½ MILES TO RANWORTH - 30 MINUTES

MOORINGS: There are a number of moorings all around Horning proper but outside the pub there is room for about 20 side on. A charge of £3 is levied on the pub side but if you moor on the other side you can be rowed over.

SUMMER:	All day
WINTER:	11 to 2.30 and 6 to 11
SUNDAY:	Noon to 10.30 in Summer
	Noon to 3 and 7 to 10.30 in Winter

BEERS:	John Smiths Smooth, Theakstons Best, Bombadier, Websters and Directors
LAGERS:	Kronenberg and Fosters

SPECIALITIES: Hot and Cold Food Servery. Breakfasts served from 9 to 10.30

SUNDAY LUNCH: Main course - £4.95

BAR MEALS: Noon to 9 pm for cold food. Lunch and Dinner - Noon to 2 and 6.30 to 9

DINING FACILITIES: Seating for 100. Times as above. Average cost of two course meal for two with wine: £21.

CARDS: All major cards and Cashback.

Built on the site of Monks' Mead House in 1840 this is one of Broadlands better known pubs.

Redevelopment during January to March 2000 has allowed for a large family area, a new bar and toilets for the disabled. There are smoking and non-smoking areas in the dining section.

Play pool outside on the patio area which is covered during inclement weather. A massive indoor games room and crazy golf are also provided. The wide doors and lack of steps make the Inn convenient for those with wheelchairs. Sorry, no dogs.

The pub suffered a direct bomb hit in 1941, killing 20 people, and was gutted in 1965 in a thatch fire.

RANWORTH

MALTSTERS   TEL: (01603) 270241

3 MILES FROM HORNING - 30 MINUTES
1 MILE TO ANT MOUTH - 20 MINUTES
3 MILES TO THURNE MOUTH - 30 MINUTES
5 MILES TO UPTON DYKE - 45 MINUTES

MOORINGS: Approximtely 20, stern on. There is no charge for the first 24 hours and the distance to the pub is 100 to 200 yards. A busy spot so moor early to avoid the rush.

SUMMER:	All day (June to August)
WINTER:	11 to 2.30 and 7 to 11
SUNDAY:	Noon to 3 and 7 to 10.30
	Noon to 10.30 in Summer

BEERS:	Theakstons Best and Mild, Directors and John Smiths Smooth
LAGERS:	Fosters and Kronenberg

SPECIALITIES: Lasagne. Beef 'n Ale pie. Beer Battered Cod. Pork 'n Leek sausages. Half a Roast Chicken. Vegetarian meals.

SUNDAY LUNCH: Roast - £4.50 plus 'Specials' Board

BAR MEALS: 11.30 to 2 and 6.30 to 9

DINING FACILITIES: Seating for 40. Times as above. Typical cost of two course meal for two with wine: £20.

CARDS: All main cards plus Cashback.

Extensive refurbishments have not detracted from the charm of this lovely old pub which was built in 1762. The split-level bar, lounge and non-smoking dining area are well decorated with comfortable seating in a relaxing atmosphere.

Background music is in keeping with the setting and a family room lies behind the old Ship's Prow which has been reconstructed at the rear of the pub. A piano is available for those who can play.

Ranworth boasts one of Broadlands most beautiful churches and if you climb to the top you are promised an excellent view. Here, also, is Broadlands Conservation Centre and Nature Trail.

UPTON DYKE

THE WHITE HORSE   TEL: (01493) 750696

5 MILES FROM RANWORTH - 45 MINUTES
3 MILES FROM THURNE MOUTH - 30 MINUTES
1 MILE TO ACLE BRIDGE - 20 MINUTES

MOORINGS: A 3 m.p.h. limit to the head of the dyke which has a turning basin at the end. Room for 10 boats moored side on, along the bank. Distance to the pub is a ten minute walk through the village. Torches necessary at night.

SUMMER:	All day
WINTER:	All day
SUNDAY:	Noon to 10.30
BEERS:	Adnams, Polly's Folly, Woodfordes Revenge, Guinness, St. Peter's Best and Guest Ales
LAGERS:	Carling Black Label and Grolsch
SPECIALITIES:	Omelettes. Garlic Mushrooms. Sirloin Steak. Sherry Trifle. Children's Menu. Vegetarian dishes.
SUNDAY LUNCH:	Roast and sweet - £4.95
BAR MEALS:	Noon to 3.30 and 7 to 9.30

DINING FACILITIES: Seating for 16 and one at the piano! Times as for bar meals. Typical cost of two course meal for two with wine: £20.

CARDS: All main cards welcome, except Amex.

Built in 1824, this pub became a Freehouse in 1993. Traditional decor right down to the wood burning stoves and a snug. Read about the "Drinker's Lament". In the raised restaurant you may well feel that time has stood still - but not for obvious reasons!

Darts are provided together with live music every Thursday night and fish and chips on Fridays. Children and dogs are welcome and there is a pretty L-shaped garden to the rear.

A free taxi service is available back to your boat if the Landlord is not too busy.

ACLE BRIDGE

THE BRIDGE   TEL: (01493) 750288

1 MILE FROM UPTON DYKE - 20 MINUTES
2 MILES TO STOKESBY - 20 MINUTES

MOORINGS: Numerous on both sides of the river. There is no charge unless you moor on certain areas west of the bridge in which case a small fee overnight is requested. Distance to pub is 75 to 200 yards. Torches useful at night.

SUMMER:	11 to 11
WINTER:	11 to 3 and 6 to 11
SUNDAY:	12 to 3 and 7 to 10.30
	Noon to 10.30 in Summer

BEERS:	Theakstons XB, Guinness, Courage Best, Directors and John Smiths Smooth
LAGERS:	Fosters and Kronenberg

SPECIALITIES: Cottage Pie. Lamb Stew and dumplings. Moussaka. Apple Crumble. Baguettes. Vegetarian Menu. Under 12s Menu for £3.

SUNDAY LUNCH: Carvery Roasts - £4.95

BAR MEALS: Noon to 2.30 and 6 to 9

DINING FACILITIES: Seating for 100 anywhere in pub and in non-smoking Dining Area. Times as above. Typical cost of two course meal for two with wine: £20.

CARDS: All main cards welcome, except Amex.

A pleasant inn, tastefully decorated and with enough staff to cope during busy times. As Acle Bridge is a fairly large "beginning and ending" area there is usually the odd hilarious tale to tell or be told.

Cold food every afternoon in Summer. Large gardens, dogs welcome and play areas for children are available, inside and out.

Pleasant background music is played and good facilities for the disabled are provided.

Don't forget to ask about the legend of the Bridge.

STOKESBY

THE FERRY INN TEL: (01493) 751096

2 MILES FROM ACLE BRIDGE – 20 MINUTES
9 MILES TO GREAT YARMOUTH – 1 1/2 HOURS

MOORINGS: On the pub side of the river there is room for 20 or so boats. A small fee for 24 hours is collected downstream by local residents. Distance to the pub is 50 to 200 yards. Keep and eye on the rise and fall of the river.

SUMMER:	All day
WINTER:	11 to 3 and 7 to 11
SUNDAY:	Noon to 3 and 7 to 10.30

BEERS:	Adnams, Whitbread Bitter, Guinness and Guest Ales
LAGERS:	Carlsberg and Stella Artois

SPECIALITIES: Wild Mushroom Lasagne. Half pound Burgers.Childrens and Vegetarians' menu.

SUNDAY LUNCH: Roasts - £5.25

BAR MEALS: Noon to 2.30 and 6 to 9.30

DINING FACILITIES: Seating anywhere. Times as above. Average cost of three course meal for two with wine: £23.

CARDS: Main cards accepted.

Long, low and rambling with a pretty garden and patio area overlooking the river, this is a genuine Olde Worlde Inn with one oak-beamed bar full of brassware, copper, pictures and general bric a brac.

The background music is not overpowering and there is a large comfortable lounge and family room. Open fires in winter months. Sorry, no dogs allowed inside.

Just behind the pub you will find a good Grocery, Gift Shop and Tea Room - open 7 days a week. Cycle Hire is available. from here. The new "Village Experience" is a short distance away.

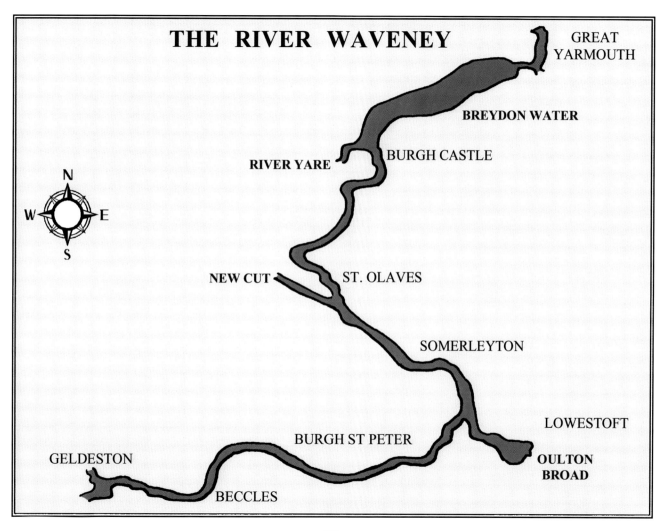

THE RIVER WAVENEY

GREAT YARMOUTH

BREYDON WATER

RIVER YARE   BURGH CASTLE

NEW CUT   ST. OLAVES

SOMERLEYTON

LOWESTOFT

BURGH ST PETER   OULTON BROAD

GELDESTON

BECCLES

THE RIVER WAVENEY - DISTANCES AND TIMINGS

BURGH CASTLE TO GELDESTON

BURGH CASTLE TO ST. OLAVES = 4 1/2 MILES - 30 MINUTES
ST. OLAVES TO NEW CUT = 1/2 MILE - 15 MINUTES
NEW CUT TO SOMERLEYTON = 1 1/2 MILES - 15 MINUTES
SOMERLEYTON TO OULTON BROAD = 5 MILES - 45 MINUTES
OULTON BROAD TO BURGH ST PETER = 3 MILES - 30 MINUTES
BURGH ST PETER TO BECCLES = 6 1/2 MILES - 1 HOUR
BECCLES TO GELDESTON = 2 1/2 MILES - 30 MINUTES

GELDESTON TO BURGH CASTLE

GELDESTON TO BECCLES = 2 1/2 MILES - 30 MINUTES
BECCLES TO BURGH ST PETER = 6 1/2 MILES - 1 HOUR
BURGH ST PETER TO OULTON BROAD = 3 MILES - 30 MINUTES
OULTON BROAD TO SOMERLEYTON = 5 MILES - 45 MINUTES
SOMERLEYTON TO NEW CUT = 1 1/2 MILES - 15 MINUTES
NEW CUT TO ST OLAVES = 1/2 MILE - 15 MINUTES
ST OLAVES TO BURGH CASTLE = 4 1/2 MILES - 30 MINUTES

THE RIVER WAVENEY

AT THE BEGINNING OF THIS RIVER LIE THE REMAINS OF BURGH CASTLE. IF YOU WISH TO VISIT FRITTON LAKE COUNTRYWORLD, WHERE THERE IS A CAFE, A NINE HOLE GOLF COURSE, FALCONRY, HORSE AND CART RIDES, FISHING, LAUNCH TRIPS AND HEAVY HORSE STABLES, THE ROAD FROM ST. OLAVES IS BEST.

ALMOST OPPOSITE ST. OLAVES IS THE NEW CUT (BUILT IN 1833), AN ALTERNATIVE ROUTE TO THE RIVER YARE. FURTHER ALONG IS AN IRON SUSPENSION BRIDGE WHICH CONNECTS NORFOLK AND SUFFOLK.

ONCE PAST SOMERLEYTON BEAR LEFT FOR OULTON BROAD. AT LOWESTOFT THERE ARE TOURS TO SEE ROUND THE FISHING TRADE ON TUESDAYS, WEDNESDAYS AND THURSDAYS FROM MID JULY TO MID SEPTEMBER. GOOD BATHING, BINGO, A PAVILION, PARKS, PIERS AND PITCH AND PUTT ARE ALSO WITHIN EASY REACH.

CRUISE ON TO BECCLES (HARBOUR PICTURED ABOVE). BUILT ON SEVERAL LEVELS, BECCLES IS A LOVELY OLD MARKET TOWN WITH A WEALTH OF ANCIENT HOUSES, GOOD SHOPS, SEVERAL PUBS, AND AN OUTSIDE HEATED SWIMMING POOL. THE CHURCH OF ST. MICHAEL, WHERE LORD NELSON'S PARENTS WERE MARRIED IN 1749, CAN BE SEEN AT QUITE A DISTANCE FROM THE RIVER.

BECCLES BRIDGE (HEIGHT AT HIGH WATER - 6'8") SHOULD ONLY BE NAVIGATED AT LOW TIDES. ON THE WAY TO GELDESTON THERE ARE MANY AREAS FOR GOOD FISHING. AT THE TOP OF THE RIVER THE RIGHT FORK LEADS TO GELDESTON VILLAGE.

ST OLAVES

THE BELL INN   TEL: (01493) 488249

4 1/2 MILES FROM BURGH CASTLE - 30 MINUTES
1/2 MILE TO NEW CUT - 10 MINUTES
7 MILES TO OULTON BROAD - 1 HOUR, 20 MINUTES

MOORINGS: Room for about 20 boats stern on. There is no charge but watch the current here and keep an eye on the ebb and flow of the river. Distance to pub is 50 to 200 yards.

SUMMER:	All day – weather permitting
WINTER:	11.30 to 3 and 6.30 to 11
SUNDAY:	Noon to 3.30 and 7 to 10.30

BEERS:	Adnams, Woodfordes Wherry, Murphys, Whitbread Best and Specials
LAGERS:	Heineken and Stella Artois

SPECIALITIES: Between 8 to 10 dishes each, of Fish, Poultry and Steak. Vegetarian and Children's Menus.

SUNDAY LUNCH: Roasts - £5.95

BAR MEALS: Noon to 2.30 and 6.30 to 9

DINING FACILITIES: Seating for 55. Times as above. Typical cost of three course meal for two with wine: £35.

CARDS: All main cards and 'Taste'.

One of Broadlands oldest Inns with 15th Century oak beams, genuine brass fittings and copper canopies. Fires are lit whenever "there's a chill in the air". A lovely split-level restaurant overlooks landscaped gardens, a pond, patio and the river beyond. Cheerful staff.

Background and outside music are provided and the service is good. Take away food and beer are available. "This Inn welcomes well behaved children and dogs on leads." Special food nights in the winter months.

The remains of 13th Century St. Olaves Priory are situated nearby and Fritton Lake Country World is a mile away from the village.

OULTON BROAD

LADY OF THE LAKE   TEL: (01502) 574740

7 MILES FROM ST OLAVES - 1 HOUR, 20 MINUTES
3 MILES TO BURGH ST PETER - 30 MINUTES

MOORINGS: Numerous stern on. Distance to the pub is 200 yards across the river bridge by the side of the Wherry. There is a charge of £5 for 24 hours.

SUMMER:	11 to 11
WINTER:	11 to 11
SUNDAY:	Noon to 10.30

BEERS:	Websters, Guinness, John Smiths and Theakstons Mild
LAGERS:	Fosters and Kronenberg

SPECIALITIES: All day Breakfast. Three Cheese Pasta Bake. Chicken Kiev. Mega Mixed Grill. Corned Beef Hash.

SUNDAY LUNCH: £3.99 (Roasts available every day)

BAR MEALS: Noon to 9

DINING FACILITIES: Seating for 60. Times as above. Average cost of three course meal for two with wine: £20.

CARDS: All main cards accepted.

A happy family pub close to the water with a pleasant patio and gardens. Bar-B-Q's are held during the summer.

There is one large bar leading into an attractive dining area with views over the Broad. Games and background music are provided and there is a children's area. Sorry, no dogs.

Spot the flood level. Ask the landlord what happened in January 1953.

Every Thursday evening, during the Summer, Oulton Broad hosts a power boat race which attracts a large number of visitors.

OULTON BROAD

WHERRY HOTEL   TEL: (01502) 516845

7 MILES FROM ST OLAVES - 1 HOUR, 20 MINUTES
3 MILES TO BURGH ST PETER – 30 MINUTES

MOORINGS: Numerous stern on. There is a 24 hour mooring charge of £5. Distance to the Hotel is 100 to 200 yards.

SUMMER:	11 to 11
WINTER:	11 to 11
SUNDAY:	Noon to 10.30

BEERS:	Abbot, Greene King, Guinness and Guest Beers
LAGERS:	Carlsberg and Stella Artois

SPECIALITIES:	Crepe Farcie. Nachos. Skillet meals. Rack of Lamb. Fillet of Salmon. Children's and Vegetarian Menus.

SUNDAY LUNCH: Carvery: Two for £10 - Noon to 9.30

BAR MEALS: Noon to 2 and 7 to 10

DINING FACILITIES: Seating for 120. Times as above. Typical cost of three course meal for two with wine: £35.

CARDS: All main cards accepted.

A large and imposing Hotel with glass and marble decor and a selection of bars, situated on the waterfront. Open plan seating allows for space and comfort. The large glass Conservatory, which overlooks Oulton Broad, is suitable for families.

A pleasant mixture of good service in a sociable and interesting setting. Background music is supplied together with various entertainment during the summer months and there is plenty of seating provided outside. Dogs are welcome.

Breakfast is available to river travellers and the Carvery is open seven days a week. On Fridays nights note, "drinks for two at the price for one."

OULTON BROAD

THE COMMODORE   TEL: (01502) 565955

7 MILES FROM ST OLAVES - 1 HOUR, 20 MINUTES
3 MILES TO BURGH ST PETER - 30 MINUTES

MOORINGS: There are 8, side on, at the pub where the charge is £3.50 per night refundable against food purchased inside. Distance to the pub is approximately 200 yards turning left up Commodore Road at the back of the Wherry.

SUMMER:	All day
WINTER:	11 to 3 and 5 to 11
SUNDAY:	Noon to 10.30 in the Summer and Noon to 3 and 5 to 10.30 in the Winter
BEERS:	John Smiths Smooth, Directors and Theakston Best
LAGERS:	Fosters and Kronenberg
SPECIALITIES:	Cheese and Broccoli Bake. Mixed Grill. Scampi. Lasagne. Fish and Chips.
SUNDAY LUNCH:	Roasts - £4.95
BAR MEALS:	11.30 to 9. Noon to 9 on Sundays

DINING FACILITIES: Seating for 38 inside with a large dining area outside. There are plans for a covered area with heating. Times as above. Average cost of two course meal for two with wine: £17.

CARDS: All major cards except Amex, plus Cashback.

Over 100 years old with one large oak beamed bar and small, secluded seating areas. Children are welcome but it is requested that dogs are kept outside. No special facilities for the disabled.

A pub in the true sense of the word. No pool table, no darts and only light background music. With its coaching lamps and pretty plates the warmth and hospitality are generated by a desire to keep this hostelry as a sociable meeting place for all.

Enjoy unrestricted views over Oulton Broad from the raised balcony dining area and the large tiered gardens reaching down to the patio area at the water's edge. Bar-B-Q's in the summer.

BURGH ST PETER

THE WAVENEY RIVER CENTRE TEL: (01502) 677343

3 MILES FROM OULTON BROAD - 30 MINUTES
6 ½ MILES TO BECCLES - I HOUR

MOORINGS: Numerous and mostly stern on. There is a charge of £4.50 after 5 p.m. for overnight mooring, with electric hook-ups. Distance to the Waveney Inn is 50 to 200 yards.

SUMMER:	11 30 to 3 and 6 to 11
WINTER:	As above. Closed in January
SUNDAY:	Noon to 3.30 and 6 to 10.30

BEERS:	Adnams, Woodfordes, Worthington Caffreys and Murphys
LAGERS:	Carling, Grolsch and Carling Premium

SPECIALITIES:	Whitebait. Beef Stroganoff. Thai Red Beef Curry. Childrens' Menu.

SUNDAY LUNCH:	Roasts - £5.95 plus main menu available

BAR MEALS:	Noon to 2.30 and 6.30 to 9

DINING FACILITIES: Seating for 90. Times as above. Typical cost of three course meal for two with wine: £33.

CARDS: Visa and Mastercard.

Pleasant and unobstrusive service in a quiet and relaxed atmosphere. A good general store and Marina facilities are provided together with an indoor complex featuring a Pool, Sauna, Spa Bath and Gym. Camping facilities, Boat hire and luxury caravan hire are also offered.

There are pleasant views across the river and fields from the bar and restaurant which is divided into smoking and non-smoking areas. Music is supplied by background tapes and there is a children's entertainment room.

Good amenities for the disabled. Sorry, no dogs.

BECCLES

BEAR AND BELLS TEL: (01502) 712291

6 ½ MILES FROM BURGH ST PETER - 1 HOUR
2 1/2 MILES TO GELDESTON - 30 MINUTES

MOORINGS: Plentiful at the main Yacht Basin where the charge is £4.50 weekdays and £6.50 at weekends for 24 hours. A five minute walk, towards the church and into Old Market Square, will take you to the pub.

SUMMER:	11 to 3 and 5.30 to 11 All day Friday and Saturday
WINTER:	11 to 3 and 5.30 to 11
SUNDAY:	Noon to 3 and 7 to 10.30
BEERS:	Very large range of Adnams and Greene King plus Guest Beers
LAGERS:	Carling Black Label and Stella Artois
SPECIALITIES:	Fillet Steak. Chilli Con Carne. Plaice stuffed with Prawns. Children's Menu.
SUNDAY LUNCH:	Roasts - £6.95 plus Main Menu.
BAR MEALS:	Noon to 2 and 6 to 9

DINING FACILITIES: Seating for 20. Times as above. Typical cost of two course meal for two with wine: £20.

CARDS: Cheque with bankers card. Card facilities due 2001.

Not featured since the first edition this Freehouse came under new ownership in September 2000.

One L-shaped bar featuring oak beams, themed World War II pictures and a fascinating collection of jugs and mugs. A 'quiet local pub'.

There is a function room available and a beer garden should be operational by Easter 2001.

*Interestingly, this Grade II listed building has been **open** as a pub since 1649. In 1815 five horses perished in a disastrous stable fire.*

BECCLES

WAVENEY HOUSE HOTEL   TEL: (01502) 712270

6 ½ MILES FROM BURGH ST PETER - 1 HOUR
2 1/2 MILES TO GELDESTON - 30 MINUTES

MOORINGS: Care is needed when navigating under the low bridge on the way to Geldeston. There is room for 6 boats if moored stern on. No charge if you are using the hotel and the distance to the pub is " over the wall" if already here, or a five minute walk from the Yacht Basin.

SUMMER:	All day (Hotel Bar)
WINTER:	All day (Hotel Bar)
SUNDAY:	Noon to 10.30

BEERS:	Adnams, Woodfordes Wherry and 6X
LAGERS:	Stella Artois and Carlsberg

SPECIALITIES: Roast Duckling. Baked Salmon Supreme topped with Prawns and Capers. Suffolk Ham.

SUNDAY LUNCH: £11.50 - 3 courses and coffee

BAR MEALS: Noon to 2 and 7 to 9

DINING FACILITIES: Seating for 60 in the Regency Restaurant. 7.30 to 9. Average cost of three course meal for two with wine: £45. Table d'hote menu for £11.50.

CARDS: All main cards accepted.

Originally a private house built circa 1592 with additions from 1750 onwards and now listed as a Grade One building.

The hotel remains open throughout the year and is designed to provide every comfort and amenity. A lovely patio area fronts onto the river and food is willingly served to you there or to your boat.

Music is provided by background tapes. Children are allowed inside the hotel but it is requested that good manners are to the fore. Dogs welcome.

Chintzy, olde worlde and comfortable this is a place to do justice to a good meal or merely entrench yourself and unwind in peace.

BECCLES

THE SWAN HOUSE   TEL: (01502) 713474

6 ½ MILES FROM BURGH ST PETER – 1 HOUR
2 1/2 MILES TO GELDESTON - 30 MINUTES

MOORINGS: Plentiful at the main Yacht Station where the charge is £4.50 weekdays and £6.50 at weekends for 24 hours. Walk up through the village and you will find the Swan House by the side of the Church in Newmarket Street.

SUMMER:	All day
WINTER:	All day
SUNDAY:	Noon to 10.30

BEERS: There are many imported beers and lagers at reasonable prices   - Adnams, St Peters and Budvar to name a few.

SPECIALITIES: Confit of Duck with exotic fruit & Cointreau sauce. Italian bread & butter pudding with Amaretto sauce. Tomato pudding with Basil .

SUNDAY LUNCH: £9.90 for 2 courses. £12.90 for 3 courses.

BAR MEALS: Noon to 2.15 and 6.45 to 9.30

DINING FACILITIES: Seating for 38. Times as above. Evening bar menu for two courses from £18.

CARDS: All cards accepted.

Definitely the place for the connoisseur of good food and wine. It is advisable to book ahead during busy times. Smoking is 'tolerated'.

A home from home with open fires, chintz settees and armchairs, round wooden tables and Chesterfields. Piles of logs lie neatly stacked and there are board games to play.

There is pleasant background music and live groups on Sundays and Mondays. Not really suitable for those with children or dogs.

If you want to know how to make up those Cork "Notice Boards" you see in the shops take a look at the Proprietors' idea!

GELDESTON

THE WHERRY (01508) 518371

2 1/2 MILES FROM BECCLES- 30 MINUTES

MOORINGS: Steer to your right at the fork. Between six and eight side on just before the cut that goes round the old disused railway bridge. There is no charge and the pub is a two minute walk away.

SUMMER:	Noon to 3 and 7 to 11
	All day Saturday
WINTER:	Noon to 3 and 7 to 11
SUNDAY:	Noon to 10.30
BEERS:	Adnams, Tetleys, Whitbread and Murphys
LAGERS:	Carlsberg and Stella Artois

SPECIALITIES: Camembert Wedges. Home-made Lasagne. Childrens' Menu.

SUNDAY LUNCH: Roasts - £5.95 plus Main Menu

BAR MEALS: Noon to 2 and 7 to 9

DINING FACILITIES: Seating for 24. Times as above. Typical cost of three course meal with wine: £25.

CARDS: Cheque with bankers card.

A 16th century building with log fires and a 'real pub' interior with old bench seats and wooden rafters. The lounge has a Swiss Chalet effect.

There is a pretty garden with ample seating, a secluded walled garden and a "secret, non-smoking, restaurant!

Children are welcome as are Dogs - inside and out. There are good facilities for the disabled. "Phat" – a Waveney Valley game is played here.

Fishing is good all round this area and there is a general store in the village. Pony trap rides are available outside in the summer months.

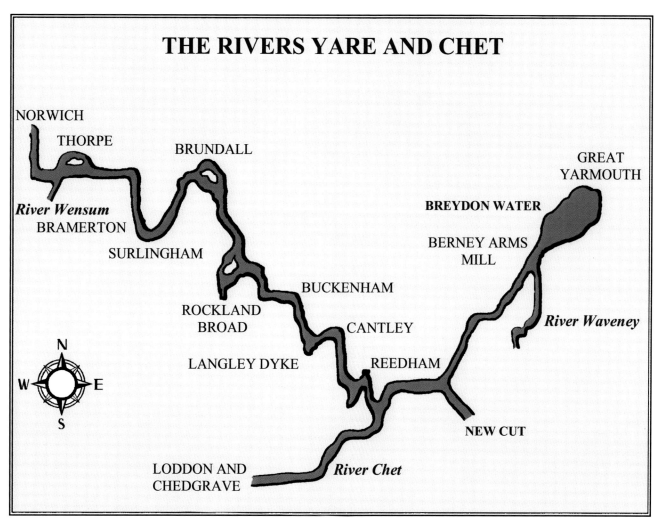

THE RIVERS YARE AND CHET

NORWICH

THORPE

BRUNDALL

GREAT YARMOUTH

BREYDON WATER

River Wensum

BRAMERTON

BERNEY ARMS MILL

SURLINGHAM

BUCKENHAM

ROCKLAND BROAD

River Waveney

CANTLEY

LANGLEY DYKE

REEDHAM

N
W E
S

NEW CUT

LODDON AND CHEDGRAVE

River Chet

THE RIVERS YARE AND CHET - DISTANCES AND TIMINGS

BERNEY ARMS MILL (BREYDON WATER) TO NORWICH YACHT STATION

BERNEY ARMS MILL TO MOUTH OF NEW CUT = 2 MILES - 20 MINUTES
MOUTH OF NEW CUT TO REEDHAM = 2 1/2 MILES - 25 MINUTES
REEDHAM TO LODDON AND CHEDGRAVE = 5 MILES - 45 MINUTES
REEDHAM TO CANTLEY = 3 MILES - 30 MINUTES
LODDON AND CHEDGRAVE TO CANTLEY = 5 MILES - 45 MINUTES
CANTLEY TO LANGLEY DYKE = 1 MILE - 15 MINUTES
LANGLEY DYKE TO BUCKENHAM = 2 MILES - 30 MINUTES
BUCKENHAM TO ROCKLAND BROAD = 2 MILES - 30 MINUTES
ROCKLAND BROAD TO SURLINGHAM = 3 MILES - 45 MINUTES
SURLINGHAM TO BRAMERTON = 3 MILES - 45 MINUTES
BRAMERTON TO THORPE = 3 MILES - 45 MINUTES
THORPE TO NORWICH YACHT STATION = 2 MILES - 30 MINUTES

NORWICH YACHT STATION TO BERNEY ARMS MILL (BREYDON WATER)

NORWICH YACHT STATION TO THORPE = 2 MILES - 30 MINUTES
THORPE TO BRAMERTON = 3 MILES - 45 MINUTES
BRAMERTON TO SURLINGHAM = 3 MILES - 45 MINUTES
SURLINGHAM TO ROCKLAND BROAD = 3 MILES - 45 MINUTES
ROCKLAND BROAD TO BUCKENHAM = 2 MILES - 30 MINUTES
BUCKENHAM TO LANGLEY DYKE = 2 MILES - 30 MINUTES
LANGLEY DYKE TO CANTLEY = 1 MILE - 15 MINUTES
CANTLEY TO LODDON AND CHEDGRAVE = 5 MILES - 45 MINUTES
CANTLEY TO REEDHAM = 3 MILES - 30 MINUTES
LODDON AND CHEDGRAVE TO REEDHAM = 5 MILES - 45 MINUTES
REEDHAM TO MOUTH OF NEW CUT = 2 1/2 MILES - 25 MINUTES
MOUTH OF NEW CUT TO BERNEY ARMS MILL = 2 MILES - 20 MINUTES

CROSSING BREYDON WATER AND THE RIVERS YARE AND CHET

CROSSING BREYDON WATER IS NOT AS DAUNTING AS IT LOOKS. ALWAYS CROSS AT LOW TIDES. YOUR ANNUAL TIDE TABLE WILL TELL YOU WHEN THESE ARE. WHEN GOING UNDER BREYDON BRIDGE TAKE CARE TO STEER UNDER THE RED AND WHITE STRIPED TRIANGLES WHICH POINT DOWN TO THE RIVER. IF THREE RED LIGHTS SHOW ON THE BRIDGE KEEP TO THE EXTREME RIGHT HAND CHANNEL. FROM GREAT YARMOUTH TO BERNEY ARMS MILL KEEP BETWEEN THE POSTS AS FOLLOWS:

RED ON YOUR LEFT (PORT) HAND SIDE.
GREEN OR BLACK WITH A WHITE TOP ON YOUR RIGHT (STARBOARD) HAND SIDE.
REVERSE THE ABOVE IF COMING TOWARDS YARMOUTH.

THE CROSSING TAKES APPROXIMATELY 1 HOUR, DEPENDANT ON TIDES. MOORING FEES AT GREAT YARMOUTH, AT THE TIME OF GOING TO PRESS, ARE £13 FOR 24 HOURS.

BERNEY ARMS MILL IS THE TALLEST IN NORFOLK, IS IN FULL WORKING ORDER AND WORTH A VISIT. THE SURROUNDING MARSHES BELONG TO THE R.S.P.B. ONCE PAST THE NEW CUT (A SHORT ROUTE TO THE RIVER WAVENEY) REEDHAM CAN BE SEEN. FURTHER ALONG WATCH OUT FOR REEDHAM CAR FERRY. THIS IS THE LAST WORKING CHAIN FERRY IN EAST ANGLIA.

THE RIVER CHET FLOWS OFF THE YARE AND WILL TAKE YOU TO LODDON AND CHEDGRAVE WHICH ARE ATTRACTIVE MARKET TOWNS.

IF YOU GO PAST THE RIVER CHET, YOU WILL SHORTLY ARRIVE AT CANTLEY WHERE THE FIRST SUGAR BEET FACTORY TO BE BUILT IN THIS COUNTRY IS STILL IN USE. THE RIVER FROM HERE TO THORPE, NEAR NORWICH, IS WIDE AND PLEASANT WITH MANY INTERESTING PUBS ON THE WAY. THORPE BRIDGES ARE 6' AND 6.2" AT HIGH WATER.

REEDHAM

THE SHIP TEL: (01493) 700287

4 1/2 MILES FROM BERNEY ARMS MILL - 30 MINUTES
5 MILES TO LODDON - 45 MINUTES
3 MILES TO CANTLEY - 30 MINUTES

MOORINGS: Three, side on, by the pub which is very near the railway bridge. There is no charge and the pub is on your 'doorstep', through the pretty gardens. Please keep an eye on the rise and fall of the river if moored overnight.

SUMMER:	11 to 11
WINTER:	11 to 2.30 and 6 to 11
SUNDAY:	Noon to 2.30 and 7 to 10.30
	Noon to 10.30 during Summer

BEERS: Adnams, Stones, Worthington Best Caffreys and Guinness

LAGERS: Carling, Tennents Extra and Grolsch

SPECIALITIES: Pate. Superb Steaks. Different daily specials. Childrens Menu from £2.50. The same Chef for the past ten years!

SUNDAY LUNCH: Roasts - £5.50

BAR MEALS: 11 to 2.30 and 6.30 to 9.30

DINING FACILITIES: Seating for 20. Times as above. Average cost of three course meal for two with wine. £25.

CARDS: Cheque with bankers card.

An interesting collection of miniatures adorn the ceiling of the lounge bar where copper canopied fireplaces and comfortable seating are much in evidence.

The restaurant boasts a very unusual selection of musical instruments and chamber pots!

There is a childrens room with amusements, background music and the occasional jazz group in summer months. Dogs allowed and there is good access for the disabled.

Reedham is an attractive village with numerous cottages, cafes and shops along the water's edge. A well known landmark is the church of St. John the Baptist.

REEDHAM

LORD NELSON
TEL: (01493) 701239

4 1/2 MILES FROM BERNEY ARMS MILL - 30 MINUTES
5 MILES TO LODDON - 45 MINUTES
3 MILES TO CANTLEY - 30 MINUTES

MOORINGS: Six to eight side on. Double mooring permitted. There is no charge if you are patrons. Distance to the pub is 25 to 50 yards. Please keep an eye on the rise and fall of the river if moored overnight. Torches useful.

SUMMER:	All day, Friday, Saturday and Sunday 11 to 3 and 6 to 11 Monday to Thursday
WINTER:	11.30 to 2.30 and 7 to 11 Closed lunchtimes on Mondays
SUNDAY:	Noon to 3 and 7 to 10.30
BEERS:	Greene King IPA, Woodfordes, John Smith Smooth and 'Humpty Dumpty' (brewed in the village!)
LAGERS:	Fosters, Kronenberg and Holsten
SPECIALITIES:	Fresh Fish, Steaks and home-made dishes.
SUNDAY LUNCH:	Roasts - £4.95 plus Bar Snacks.
BAR MEALS:	Noon to 2 and 7 to 9

DINING FACILITIES: Seating for 40. Times as above. Typical cost of three course meal for two with wine: £32.

CARDS: All major cards accepted.

"Welcome to our Home" says the sign outside and the atmosphere within represents that. Your hosts were regional winners of the British Institute of Innkeepers in 1999. Recently renovated the pub is owned by the Vintage Hallmark Ale Company.

There is one large bar with a pleasant dining room to your left which overlooks the river.

Children are welcome and there are open fires and musical evenings. Only Guide dogs allowed and there are limited facilities for the disabled.

Pettits Farm is a ten minute walk from here. Sadly their 'fun bus' does not run anymore.

LODDON

THE SWAN INN   TEL: (01508) 520239

5 MILES FROM REEDHAM - 1 HOUR
3 MILES TO LANGLEY DYKE - 30 MINUTES

MOORINGS: Plentiful at the Staithe - mostly stern on. There is no charge. Turn left by the Bridge and the Swan is a three minute stroll away, opposite the Church.

SUMMER:	11 to 11
WINTER:	11 to 11
SUNDAY:	Noon to 10.30

BEERS: Adnams, Whitbread Best and Mild, Boddingtons, Murphys, Castle Eden, Wadsworth 6X and Guinness

LAGERS: Stella Artois and Heineken

SPECIALITIES: Chicken Orleans. Roast Rack of Lamb. Death by Chocolate. Burgers of every type and size. Childrens' Menu

SUNDAY LUNCH: Roasts - £4.95 plus full Menu

BAR MEALS: 11.30 to 2.30 and 6.30 to 9.30

DINING FACILITIES: Seating for 20. Times as above. Average cost of three course meal for two with wine: £35.

CARDS: All main cards except for Amex and Diners.

This is a delightful 17th/18th Century Coaching Inn. A non-smoking bar is now provided where you can also dine.

There is a pool table and video machines together with a function room upstairs. Plenty of seating outside for those hot days. Children and dogs are welcome. Good access for the disabled.

Music is supplied by background tapes and a juke box. A market is held every Monday in the pub car park.

It is anticipated that a Beer Garden will be open in 2001. 'Take away food' is available.

CHEDGRAVE

WHITE HORSE INN   TEL: (01508) 520250

5 MILES FROM REEDHAM - 1 HOUR
3 MILES TO LANGLEY DYKE - 30 MINUTES

MOORINGS: Moorings as for Loddon. Turn right and the pub is a two minute walk on the left hand side, just past the garage.

SUMMER: 11.30 to 11
WINTER: As above but subject to change so please call ahead
SUNDAY: Noon to 10.30

BEERS: Bass, Adnams, Youngs, Greene King IPA, Boddingtons Cask, Guiness and Whitbread Mild
LAGERS: Carlsberg and Stella Artois

SPECIALITIES: Steak, Onions, Fried Tomatoes, Mushrooms, Chips or Jacket Potato, Baked beans or Peas - all for £7.50

SUNDAY LUNCH: Roast Pork, Beef, Lamb or Chicken. Two Courses for £6

BAR MEALS: 12.30 to 2.30 and 6 to 9.30

DINING FACILITIES: Seating for 30. Times as above. Average cost of two course meal for two with wine: £15.

CARDS: All main cards plus Cashback.

Under new ownership and completely redecorated in March 2000 this is a Cask Marque accredited pub. Pleasant, friendly staff make for a warm and welcoming atmosphere.

There is a large garden with a sheltered Patio and it's own Bowling Green and with frequent Bar-B-Qs in the summer and roaring log fires in the winter there is something for everyone.

Children and dogs are welcome and there are good facilities for the disabled. It is requested that you do not smoke in the dining room.

Dominoes, Cribbage, Bar Skittles, Shove-Ha'penny and Scrabble are always available and a large function room for over 100 can be booked.

CANTLEY

THE RED HOUSE   TEL: (01493) 700801

3 MILES FROM REEDHAM - 30 MINUTES
5 MILES FROM LODDON - 45 MINUTES
3 MILES TO BUCKENHAM - 30 MINUTES

MOORINGS: There are between 20 to 30 side on. Further down, a small fee for overnight mooring is collected by local farmers. Distance to the pub is 50 to 100 yards.

SUMMER:	All day
WINTER:	All day
SUNDAY:	Noon to 10.30

BEERS: Tetleys, Ansells Best, Murphys, Guinness, Caffreys and Greene King IPA

LAGERS: Carlsberg and Stella Artois

SPECIALITIES: Minced Beef & Onion Pie. Spaghetti Bolognese. Bakewell Tart. Childrens' and Vegetarians' Menu.

SUNDAY LUNCH: Main menu available

BAR MEALS: Noon to 2 and 7 to 9

DINING FACILITIES: Seating anywhere in the pub. Times as above. Typical cost of a three course meal for two with wine: £15.

CARDS: Cheque with bankers card.

A sprawling Freehouse with fruit machines, juke boxes, background music, a dart board, pool table, TV, pinball and a piano. Look out for the Giant Plated lizard!

A beer garden runs alongside the pub and there are seats outside overlooking the river. Small children are safe from the river in a protected play area and dogs are welcome - "if they don't bite and are on leads". 'Take-Away" menu.

The Legend outside (a little faded now) reads: "Good wine, a friend, or being dry, or lest we should be by and by, or any other reason why ".

BUCKENHAM FERRY

BEAUCHAMP ARMS   TEL: (01508) 480247

2 MILES FROM LANGLEY DYKE - 20 MINUTES
2 MILES TO ROCKLAND BROAD - 30 MINUTES

MOORINGS: Either side of the pub will accommodate 40 comfortably side or stern on. There is no charge and the distance to the pub is 25 to 50 yards. Torches may be useful if moored a little way from the pub.

SUMMER:	All day
WINTER:	Noon to 3 and 7 to 11
	All day Saturday and Sunday
SUNDAY:	Noon to 10.30
BEERS:	Tetleys, IPA, Woodfordes Norkie and Wherry, Guinness & Ind Coope Mild
LAGERS:	Carlsberg and Carlsberg Export
SPECIALITIES:	Smoked Salmon and Mackerel. Frogs Legs. Shark Steak. Bouillabaisse. Rack of Ribs. Childrens' Menu.
SUNDAY LUNCH:	Carvery - £5.95. 2 Courses - £7.95
BAR MEALS:	11 to 3 and 7 to 9 (all day in Summer)

DINING FACILITIES: Seating for 50. Times as above. Typical cost of three course meal for two with wine: £35.

CARDS: All main cards except Amex.

A change in ownership has now led to this freehouse having the added advantage of four bedrooms complete with en-suite jacuzzi.

A family pub cum hotel with comfortable decor, good service and an attractive (non-smoking) restaurant with pleasant views of the river.

Two pool tables plus a childrens room with games and video machines are provided, together with an outside play area and a new Patio. Good access for the disabled. Dogs allowed on leads.

ROCKLAND BROAD

THE NEW INN   TEL: (01508) 538395

2 MILES FROM BUCKENHAM FERRY - 30 MINUTES
4 MILES TO SURLINGHAM - 45 MINUTES

MOORINGS: Room for about 15 boats stern on. There is no charge and the pub is 25 to 100 yards away. Torches may be useful at night.

SUMMER:	11 to 3 and 6.30 to 11
	All day Saturday & Sunday
WINTER:	11 to 3 and 6.30 to 11 (All day Saturday)
SUNDAY:	Noon to 3 and 7 to 10.30

BEERS: Bass, Tetleys, Youngs, Murphys, MB and Guest Ales

LAGERS: Carling Black Label and Carlsberg

SPECIALITIES: Moules Mariniere. Poached Norwegian Salmon. 10 oz Sirloin Steak. Good selection of Vegetarian food.

SUNDAY LUNCH: Roasts - £5.50

BAR MEALS: Noon to 2 and 7 to 9

DINING FACILITIES: Seating for 34. Times as above. Average cost of three course meal for two with wine: £23.

CARDS: All main cards except Amex.

Under new ownership since the last edition. An appealing and restful stopover in a quiet and peaceful backwater of the Broads.

An extremely clean interior with historical pictures of the Broads round the walls. Attractive beer gardens and various alterations have greatly enhanced this Inn. There is a no-smoking dining room.

A fine selection of malt and blended whisky is on offer. A family room is provided as is "take away food". Dogs welcome, parties catered for and ensuite Bed & Breakfast is now available. Please call ahead for details.

SURLINGHAM

COLDHAM HALL TAVERN   TEL: (01508) 538591

3 MILES FROM ROCKLAND BROAD – 30 MINUTES
3 MILES TO BRAMERTON – 30 MINUTES

MOORINGS: Approximately 25 stern on. There is no charge. and the pub is 50 to 100 yards away across the lawns.

SUMMER:	Noon to 11
WINTER:	Noon to 3 and 6 to 11
SUNDAY:	Noon to 10.30

BEERS:	IPA, Abbot and two changing Guest Ales
LAGERS:	Stella Artois, Carlsberg and Fosters

SPECIALITIES: Mouthwatering Steak and Kidney pies. Large Cod and Chips. Fenland Ham. Children's Menu.

SUNDAY LUNCH: Roasts - £7.95 for three courses

BAR MEALS: Noon to 2 and 6 to 9

DINING FACILITIES: Seating for 40 anywhere in the pub. Times as above. Average cost of a two course meal for two with wine: £12.

CARDS: All cards except Amex.

A beautifully appointed tavern with ivy covered walls and a large patio area which is floodlit at night. Unwind here in tranquil surroundings and the homely atmosphere provided by the staff.

The non-smoking restaurant has recently been completely renovated and offers lovely views of the river. Children welcome, as are dogs. Good facilities for the disabled.

Pool and darts are available in a separate area and the patio garden, with seating overlooking the water, is always popular on sunny days.

BRAMERTON

THE WOODS END   TEL: (01508) 538899

**2 MILES FROM SURLINGHAM - 30 MINUTES
4 MILES TO THORPE - 45 MINUTES**

MOORINGS: Room for about 20, side on, to your left alongside the pub. There is no charge.

SUMMER: 11 to 11

WINTER: November to February closed lunchtimes except for Weekends. 6.30 to 11 evenings.

SUNDAY: Noon to 10.30 in Summer
Noon to 3 & 7 to 10.30 in Winter

BEERS: Caffreys and Guinness plus "Guess it yourself" beers from all over the country. Try the following out for size! Heatwave, Decadence and No Stopping.

LAGERS: Stella Artois, Carling and Grolsch

SPECIALITIES: Beef and Guinness. Chilli Bowls. Freshly baked Baguettes. Loads of traditional home-cooked food.

SUNDAY LUNCH: Carvery - £5.95

BAR MEALS: Noon to 2 and 7 to 9

DINING FACILITIES: Seating for 40. Times as above. Average cost of three course meal for two with wine. £30.

CARDS: All main cards accepted.

A warm welcome back to this Freehouse built circa 1885. Pleasant gardens with childrens' play area. No dogs allowed. Disco on Sunday nights. Pool Table. Cream Teas, Boat Trips and Bar-B's.

Limited facilities for the disabled. An upstairs 'no-smoking' restaurant is open in the evenings only. A Fish 'n' Chip Shop operates between 4 and 7 on Friday, Saturday and Sunday.

*Ten minutes from Norwich City Centre, bed and breakfast is available at the pub. Indeed, **all** functions are catered for. Call ahead for details. Go to Woods End and "drink the fridge"!*

THORPE

THE RUSHCUTTERS   TEL: (01603) 435403

4 MILES FROM BRAMERTON - 45 MINUTES
2 MILES TO NORWICH - 30 MINUTES

MOORINGS: Room for about 15 boats moored side on. There is no charge and the pub is 25 to 50 yards away. Navigate carefully under the Bridges and check the tidal ebb and flow if stopping for long.

SUMMER:	11 to 11
WINTER:	11 to 11
SUNDAY:	Noon to 10.30

BEERS: Theakstons, John Smiths Smooth, Guinness, Directors and Guest Ales

LAGERS: Fosters and Kronenberg

SPECIALITIES: Sausage, Bubble & Squeak. Lemon Sole Braised Kidneys and Shallots. Garlic Sardines. Childrens' Menu.

SUNDAY LUNCH: Roasts (until they run out) - £6.65 plus Main Menu

BAR MEALS: 11 to 10. Noon to 9.30 Sunday

DINING FACILITIES: Seating anywhere in pub. Times as above Typical cost of three course meal for two with wine: £28.

CARDS: All main cards and Cashback.

Thorpe St. Andrew is known as the Richmond of Norfolk and, here, in this spacious hostelry everything is provided for the family.

The bars and parts of the dining areas overlook the river and there is a vast Patio area outside, from where you can watch the world go by.

In the 18th Century a rail crash resulted in the place being used as a temporary morgue. Before the Rushcutters was a public house it was a Coaching Inn and before that a Monastery. The ghost of a monk is still frequently seen!

THORPE

THE RIVER GARDEN   TEL: (01603) 703900

4 MILES FROM BRAMERTON - 45 MINUTES
2 MILES TO NORWICH - 30 MINUTES

MOORINGS: Room for three side on outside the pub (free if dining) and plenty a little further down along the river bank. Carefully under either Bridge and watch the tides.

SUMMER:	All day
WINTER:	All day
SUNDAY:	Noon to 10.30

BEERS:	Boddingtons and Adnams
LAGERS:	Heineken and Stella Artois

SPECIALITIES: Thai Star Fishcakes with Smashed Avocado. Crispy Chilli Chicken. Lamb Shank.

SUNDAY LUNCH: Roasts - £6.95

BAR MEALS: Noon to 9 - Monday to Wednesday
Noon to 10 p.m. rest of week.
Sunday - Noon to 9

DINING FACILITIES: Seating anywhere in pub or no-smoking restaurant. Times as above. Typical cost of three course meal for two with wine: £38.

CARDS: All main cards accepted.

Under new management for the past couple of years this pub was originally known as the Kings Head. Pleasantly furnished with friendly yet unobtrusive service in a relaxing atmosphere. Dogs and children welcome. Good facilites for the disabled.

Secluded landscaped gardens - now with a heated Patio for diners - slope to the river and are overlooked by the King's Room which is used for private functions. For lovers of a 'good grape' there is a large selection of wines.

History tells us that the King's Head sustained slight damage from enemy action in 1944. The pub dates back to 1700 and has known over thirty two Landlords to date.